FOR ALL THE TIMES

A COLLECTION OF LOVE POETRY

NEERAJ KUMAR

For all the lovers.

Contents

Contents

Contents

About The Book

This poetry book, "For all the Times," as the title suggests, has been written as a humble token of gratitude for all the blissfulness that the poet has got to experience in his life in the sector of romantic love.

Through this book, Neeraj Kumar, as an optimistic young poet, has tried to appreciate and celebrate all the blissful moments of love that his life has showered on him.

He has woven all the poems in sync with each other such that they flow as continued verses rather than separate stand-alone poems going haphazardly in different directions.

Unlike other poetry books, here the language of the poems is deliberately kept simple, clear, and respectful so that everyone can easily understand and feel the poems without any language restrictions.

Enjoy!

Foreword

I am thrilled with the insights and perspectives gleaming on each poem and hence, I consider it my privilege to write this foreword for 'For all the Times'

It is unusual for an author of a business self-help book to agree to write a foreword for an anthology on love. Do you think love and business are not connected? Love for customers helps business to grow. Deeper love results in businesses flourishing. Products are created with a customer persona in mind. Keeping someone in mind, identifying their likes, dislikes, challenges and adapting is common to continuance of both businesses and love. Such a person in a customer persona need not even exist. Yet a fictional profile can bring out the best from both business and a form of art like poetry.

Love is wrongly assumed to be a passing cloud in the youthful phase. Love brings in maturity for the rest of the life. When love graduates to unconditional love, an ordinary person qualifies to be called noble.

I know Neeraj over three years as a poet with versatility and an author with amazing clarity in articulation. The author brings out the prerequisite for love beautifully in this verse --

It is easy to take
something,
But to get it,
One needs to deserve it.
To win someone's heart

requires honesty,

purity and concerns unspoken.

There are several quote-worthy verses from this noteworthy young poet.

Interestingly, the top ranked questions to Alexa in 2019 from Indian users were "Will you marry me?" and "Alexa, how are you?". At the outset, these questions can be perceived as crazy and amusing. Yet interactions such as these buttress the fact that the highest form of love does not require reciprocation.

Think through most conflicts that arise between people and entities. You will agree that a majority of them spring up due to a lack of transparency and trust. Openness in intent and readiness to serve can resolve any conflict. I was startled to see this solution hidden in cryptic verse such as this in this book.

when you need me

look into my eyes

and peep into my soul.

This book titled 'For all the Times' is refreshing and distinctive.

While there are a plethora of fiction books on love, a book that preaches the fundamental essence of love in its broadest dimension is a need of the hour.

Recent research has concluded that people in love are found to have a surge of dopamine. Dopamine is connected with energy and, focus. Hypothalamus, a region of the brain considered the control center for love is associated with decision making too. I am delighted that this author has made a right decision to write a book exclusively on love covering various aspects.

Even though Love is mainstream it is sidelined quite often. Had this been an anthology on a multitude of themes, these graceful facets of love could have been overshadowed. If it happened to Tirukkural, the greatest work in classical Tamil, it could have befallen this book too. While Tirukkural has chapters 109 to 133 dedicated to love, it is repositioned or rather pigeonholed into a book on virtues. Rarely, does a speaker quote on love from Tirukkural.

If something is to bring out the best in an individual, it should be powerful and it should establish a deep personal connect. Love as in romance begins with one and expands its boundaries. Love with an individual when transpiring to wedlock, the scope of love expands to accepting a number of people in the other family and their friends too and showering love on them.

More than falling in love with someone, Neeraj has fallen in love with poetry. The alluring artistry with articulation in every poem repeatedly reinforces that Neeraj's love for poetry stands taller than his love for a mysterious woman.

What kind of a feeling can this book leave with a reader like you? I am sure it will stir up not just your feelings, but your perception of love. To put it in the poet's own words you will experience, *'I am fluttering from the inside '*.

- Dr. Venkat Kumaresan, March 1, 2023

Workplace Challenges Guru| Keynote speaker | Humorist| Coach| Poet

Author of Amazon US No.1 New Release, 'Father Of Your Team'

Acknowledgements

This book would not have materialized without the support of **Shyam Kumar**, a very dear friend of mine for almost a decade now. And **Rajendra Krishan Sir** (The founder of www.boloji.com) for his timeless guidance despite the physical distance between us (He lives in New York while I live in Delhi.) which helped me a lot not only in improving my writing but also in becoming a better person. Also, I am thankful to all my beta readers and the precious input you all provide.

Preface

This book is my tribute to all the good times. While there are several books in the market that discuss separation and life problems. I always wanted to write a book about union that has some happy vibes for the reader to read and feel good about. I personally strongly adhere to the idea that writing need not always focus on the problems, or that one need not have to go through some pain in order to write; rather, one can equally well express oneself by being jovial and full of happiness inside. May my words bring a smile to your face while you read. Cheers to all the good times! Happy Reading.

Neeraj Kumar
March 1, 2023

1. A GIFT OF JOY

From the pen which flows beauty,
I will write down your name!
From the dewdrops on the leaves,
To the silent voice in my ears,
To the rain, to the wind, to the clouds,
To the lover's eyes (yours)
I owe this joy, this smile to my face!
Making me beautiful
Like an artwork,
Like a painting drawn,
Like a poem written on my soul
giving me pleasure from within.
Just maybe or I should be assured,
This smell of ripe mangoes,
This sweet voice of cuckoo,
This entire environment vibes in order
To make me feel ageless!
Full of inner joy, painless!
Making me feel light as feathers,
I walk but I want to dance,
I talk but I want to laugh,
This gift of joy from

FOR ALL THE TIMES

the heaven's brink outpouring,
Now making me feel so alluring,
And so you're a sight for my sore eyes
which I just can't help but adore!

2. APPRECIATION

Like a fragrance that lingers,
What it is that envelops me
while I am in your presence?
Why all other people and things seem
to be ordinary and faded
in front of your effortless presence?
Even in dullness, there is freshness
A connection.
For I have felt and realized,
How amazing things can be
just by being with you.
I talk to a lot of people
but never do I feel the same
as I do with you.
Glad that our friendship is blossoming,
Let's see it unfold more.

3. TRUE COMPANIONSHIP

Yes, I know
The blissful moments
of companionship,
When joy flows
In the veins so palpable!
Do you know it?
Have you felt it?
A mutual concern!
For real?
It has its own vitality
That sprouts life
Into one's life,
One gets beholden
by the moments golden
feeling the emotions
so well perceived,
And feel the bond
which never leaves its grace,
Rather leaves a smile at our faces
Every time,

NEERAJ KUMAR

We two,
Come together.

• 5 •

4. REMINISCENCE

Some memories
leave an imprint on us
in such a way that,
It stays alive in us
even after it is long gone.
Be it a song we often listen to,
A place we visited,
Or a person we have known.
Which brings back memories.
Beauty sometimes unveils itself
In the moments,
When we are grateful.
So many people we meet,
So many things we do,
So many memories we create,
But only a few stays along.
Only a few touch
and melt our hearts......Right away!

5. A CONNECTION

There is a feather behind her ear
But it takes a man to notice,
Who knows how to tickle,
Who knows from where
Smiles on her face appear
Even knowing her to be naive
Feels her to be so appealing
The way the two attune
and end up rolling
laughing on the floor,
And feel blessed discovering,
A connection so pure.
Moments to cherish,
In the memories
Never to perish,
Rather they become,
like a thing of beauty,
A joy forever, and a day.

6. KNOWING SOMEONE WELL ENOUGH

There is always a bliss in
knowing someone well enough.
You know the small details,
The way they would behave,
Which brings smiles to your face.
All the inside jokes come alive,
That only you two understand.
Makes you two feel connected
despite the place and situation,
and feel simply blessed!

7. BLESSED MEMORIES

Like a flower, water sprinkled
and the wind flowing coolly,
Like my hair that are wet
and a heart that is now
fluttering with laughter,
A weather so fine,
A mood so swell,
Happiness, that is now
Overflowing
From within.
There are indeed some blessed memories
Lived together,
Moments
When we were glad and noticed
How joy within like a coffee brew,
Lights our faces,
Makes us bare,
So freely we tend to share,
Without much thought or care,
Like dancing in the rain,

FOR ALL THE TIMES

Drenched from head to toe,
A rainbow from within!

8. A TRUE SIGN

I know
the moments
when,
My affections great
were laid bare in front of you,
Were shown in my actions,
Unspoken, but so loud,
Made my heart melt
and then beat
faster as a drum.
A true sign
that you indeed matter a lot to me.
A hand was then shaken with faith,
To solidify us together
then and there
in a bond
that is
never meant
to be broken
but is to last till,
Forever and a day.

9. SOUVENIR

In the river of pure sentiments
we bathe and cleanse ourselves,
To keep it as a souvenir
the recollection
of the grateful moments
spent together.
A memory ever warm in time.
A mark of purity,
of being true
to each other.
Lived,
To cherish,
To be thankful
And feel forever grateful,
To be able to share,
This life along,
With each other.

10. WHAT IS IT?

A peace,
Serenity,
A joy hidden,
A feeling brimming,
Adding colors to a sketch,
As if adding ink in plain water,
As if someone whispering in my ears,
A guiding light,
A secret found,
Like a flute playing in the mist,
Like as if a drug taken
To calm, soothe
The anxiety.
A scene imprinted
Inside my mind,
Is it an illusion of perfection?
Or a divine intervention
By God above,
Through your blessed eyes?
Slow paced movements
one can feel the peace
lying within

never felt before
at any place,
in any person!
What is it?
Love?

11. PROOF

Oh,
Look me in the eye,
Do I know nothing?
Or lately,
Have I started to know everything?
Proof is the gladness that I feel in my heart,
Proof is the glow on my skin,
Proof is the coolness which I feel inside,
A place from where, this smile on my face comes in.
Proof is that I am fluttering from the inside yet I'm still.
Proof is that now I couldn't anymore hide.
Proof is that in your presence, peace I find.
Proof is that, these days I am smiling through my eyes.
Proof is that despite the season to me this weather
seems so nice.
Proof is that I always stay by your side.
Proof is that now I glow
like a guiding light.
Proof is that my life is now a bliss,
An endless fruit,
So ripe!
Now it's cooler,

Not because it's winter season,
Now it's quite peaceful,
Not because it's church region,
Rather the truth is,
It's the glimpse of your face
which is making this world
look beautiful in my view,
Or is it you,
Whom I have mistaken for my world?
Whatever the case is,
The moment I found you by my side,
I got to know how to live life!

12. BAPTIZED

So, this is how the words unfold
and the stories begin -
When impressions are made
like fresh dew drops
on our hearts.
We hear a voice,
A lovely word or two,
Heartfelt,
Like being baptized,
Away from all the sins
in the godforsaken world
that draws one's attention
towards it.
Like,
Catching someone off guard,
Leaving them in awe and wonder,
Spellbound,
One gravitates towards
the alluring unknown,
To solve the mystery,
To find the puzzle clue,
Or to simply know the truth

that shows the visions
and a possibility
of a future bright with them.
Like finding a ray of hope
for the one who is astray,
Or a home for the homeless,
Giving meaning to one's life!

13. FALLING IN LOVE

It is not quite specific
what someone would fall for,
What will make one's heart skip a beat.
Little details about someone,
which makes one's heart melt,
Which keeps on unfolding
on and on
for someone.
One can't question or ask
the reasons why,
Nor could one explain precisely
to be honest.
For one never knows,
For one never decides,
To fall in love with someone.
It rather comes on its own
as a sweet realization
in our hearts.

14. UNAVOIDABLE BEAUTY

Like a rainbow of seven colors
your joy palpable I feel in my veins
when you are around.
It is so hard to ignore the truth
for the sake of its preservation,
For I never want to lose you.
So many times, I have tried and failed
in my attempt to not notice your grace.
But the world has its own terms and conditions,
We accept what we do not want
to preserve the glimpses of
what yet could be…
Ah, have you noticed how
you always find me by your side
despite the time and situations?
A true understanding of yours,
to make the good, dazzlingly brilliant
and an antidote to alleviate the pain if any.
I know you like the way
a pencil sketch knows colors,

For I have felt beauty
in all the ways
you have continued to be
<u>Just the way you are!</u>

15. DIMENSION

A sacred dimension appears
when I am in your presence
It is this realisation
that makes me believe
in the possibility
of what yet could be.
Am I in delusion?
I hope not!
For I know,
What it feels
when faith sprouts
making one dissolve
and become one
with the other.
All it needs
is
your sanctity.

16. GRACE

I have felt grace
in the moments precious,
Like a film being played
over my eyes.
I have seen you
at the times when,
Your eyes shined
and words flowed,
Without any restraint
or fear in your mind.
I knew that I have known you when,
I saw an innocent purity gleaming in your eyes,
When I saw you through,
Like the way you see the wine
in a transparent glass from outside.
At that time, you spoke from your heart,
And I heard from that of mine.
What an instant connection!
Don't need any selection,
When we give someone
enough liberty to be
Just themselves.

17. SEEDS OF TRUST

In the times when you know me,
In the times when we are true,
It is in these times when,
Our inner affections brew.
An honest statement that we make,
The times when we don't pretend,
For you know that I am true,
For you have seen life,
For you know what it takes
To live by virtue,
A pillar of trust.
It is in these times that,
The seeds of trust are sown,
To grow into a garden whole,
That envelops us into it, for life!
An invisible warmth
we both can feel
inside our hearts
which brings with itself
years of trust,
And a bond
never to be broken,

Despite the pangs
that one endures.

18. GRATITUDE

It is easy to take
something,
But to get it,
One needs to deserve it.
To win someone's heart
requires honesty,
purity and concerns unspoken.
To do but never show,
To do for the sake of it,
To never desire to get it,
But to get it naturally
by the other.
There is no calculator
but our heart,
Which measures
the affections true.
**"Gratitude" is an overflowing gesture
of a melting heart.**

19. FORGING BONDS

Perhaps I know,
What makes one trust
and believe in the other.
Warmth felt in the heart.
A sensitivity that reaches out,
Gives a hand when needed, unasked,
Understands one inside out
and makes the other glad and grateful
in turn.
True respect and trust are earned,
Forges the bond between two
that remains unshaken,
Despite what anyone says.

20. TAKE MY HAND (BOY)

Take my hand
like a rock to lean on,
Feel my strength
find me by your side
when you need me
look into my eyes
and peep into my soul.
Do I need to say anything?
Oh,
Do I know you?
Do I understand?
How you feel
from the inside
Ask yourself!
Where there is trust,
Where there is reliability,
Where there is a promise made,
There,
You will find yourself
as if lifted and put on feathers,

As if flowers growing among weeds,
As if blooming from the inside,
Filled with the colors warm,
From an empty canvas,
To a beautiful sketch.
There,
You will find me,
As an artist
for your soul,
For you are
my art!
Brick by brick
we build
our bond.
Remember,
It's brick by brick.
On the assurance of
a brick given by you,
I give a brick.
Together with putting
hands-on hands,
Slowly and gradually
we create a place
for ourselves,
<u>We call it home.</u>

21. A CONSCIOUS CHOICE

Above smiles and mere laughter
there lies something,
Something that allows one
to give his hand,
To dance together with someone
in the journey of one's life.
Loyalty sprouts
from concern and sacrifice,
By being there for someone
in times of need.
Respect earned,
Gratitude felt,
A reason
which compels one
to payback,
Melts our heart
and forms a bond,
Which is invincible,
Which is beyond the season's change,
Which is beyond what may come!

Then we can say
By standing side by side,
By boldly coming in front,
That,
"I will take a bullet for you first if needed."
That friendship lives,
That relationship matters,
And not the one where
there is an empty laughter
without concern for each other.
Listen,
Here is the secret
For every word that we utter
its action must back it up
That is done,
Not to impress
but
out of genuine concern.
Check if they respect you,
Not only on certain conditions,
Or as per their situations suitable,
But always, out of gratitude,
Otherwise, it's just politics.
Fooling the other to take advantage,
By deceiving them.
Friends and Partners on whom we can count on
are blessings given by God,

For us to compare
the reliability of
all the other bonds
that we share with others.
Let's make a conscious choice
based on the actions of the other,
Whether to give our hand,
Whether to dance together or not,
In the journey of our life.

22. LOVE BECOMES BLIND

Everyone has got a choice
to choose to be with
whom they find nice,
But I ask,
Do we ever throw away our child?
That's what love is,
Blind!
You know
where loyalty is found,
There our love becomes blind.
Blind to the shortcomings
of the one
whom we consider,
A part of us,
Never apart from us.
We help them grow
rather asking them to change
Who they truly are,
Maybe afar in the distance,
But never ever distant

FOR ALL THE TIMES

from our heart.

• 34 •

23. TRUST

An emotion,

A feeling,

Which fills the heart

with warmth of sunlight

and forges a bond

between two hearts.

A feeling of safety,

A feeling of reliability,

And a feeling of faith in the heart

that brings trust for the other.

It takes a character

to win someone's trust

and never break it.

A place where we can fall backwards blindly

with our eyes closed,

Without even a hint of hesitation.

Such a reliability,

Such a trust,

Such a surrender,

Is won by a heart that is honest.

Honesty is not being naive rather

it is the extent of our reliability,

How trustworthy we are as a person.
Isn't it sacred?
How we let someone see us through,
To read us like a book,
Inside out
completely.
Aren't the bridges that we build
between one another's heart
are sacred paths craved?
Isn't it a privilege
to be able to allow someone
to walk on it and for the other to walk on it?
Like a secret door now slowly opening,
To let the other, enter into a dimension,
To see a version of us that we
Oh, so seldom reveal,
Which shrinks in,
In the blink of an eye,
Whenever if clouds of doubts
seems to surround.
All the beautiful tender things of the world
asks one to be sensitive first.
To know
How to handle it?
How to care?
How to love?
First,

On the reliability of which,
The flower buds slowly open,
And when opened
become
like a sunflower
to follow the directions of the sun
that is now shining bright in front of it.

24. A RIVER TAMED

As the sweet flower of gratitude
blossoms in your heart,
Crumble under the faith
you have built up on me so far.
Hush! stay silent,
Just let me know
the place where
so elegantly you hide
all of your scars,
While I swear by the same river
which you hold back in your eyes

.

.

.

That I won't ever,
Let it flow again.
(Here river is a metaphor for tears)

25. THE GIRL IN YOU

You trust in me,
I know that you do,
You know that,
Besides everything,
What others perceive
I can see,
The girl in you.
The emotional girl.
The sensible girl.
The girl who is good at heart.
The girl who is honest and bare.
Maybe you feel that
I care and understand you.
But that is for given,
For you trust me,
I know that you do,
For I girl, can feel,
The girl in you.
From the depths of your despair,
I will come as a ray of hope.
From the person you fear to be,
I will come and show you that you can.

From the place of darkness
I will light the candle of faith.
To turn your fears and doubts
To Self-Confidence,
A Head Held High.
Your eyes are oceans deep, yes
Let me sink in,
To reach out,
To find you out.

26. WE UNDERSTAND EACH OTHER

I am all ears,
Lay out all your fears,
I will mend you
where you are broken.
I feel you, I admire you,
The way you have survived.
But for a while,
Lower down your guard
and be bare,
As I am here,
For you to care.
Peel one by one
all your layers,
As my deep understanding
advances its gears,
To the point I know,
All of you,
And you know,
All of me.
Our souls intertwine,

FOR ALL THE TIMES

We two become one
and now we understand each other,
Together we may even bring out
the mesmerizing rainbows
in scorching hot summers.

27. A COMPATIBILITY

A Handshake

Of Faith,

Of Trust,

Of No Fear,

Of being there,

In times of need,

With no questions

of doubts in the mind,

But as if,

Answers of clarity

were being given,

Straight from the shrine,

To bless we two

in a unison,

In a compatibility,

To give such an understanding

of the other,

Such that,

We never need

to explain us,

But are rather understood,

FOR ALL THE TIMES

**On our own.**

28. TRUSTED

When people actually begin to trust us,
Something magical happens.
Their guard drops in,
Their "persona" vanishes,
Leaving them behind
pure and childlike.
They stop pretending to behave
and start being themselves
around us.
They tell us,
How they actually feel,
What they feel,
When they feel.
They let us see,
their real selves!
Oh, do you notice?
I bet you can feel the difference,
In their voice tone,
In their attention,
In their smile,
When they smile
through their eyes

while they talk.
You can then tell for sure
that,
You have known them,
For real.

29. TAKE MY HAND (GIRL)

I remember
you care
wishing me well
adoring.
Out of love,
Out of your kindness,
Out of a concern,
That is pure.
In the tone of my voice
out of sheer gratitude
felt in the heart within,
It can be heard.
And can be seen
in the sparkle of my eyes
that shines out in gratitude.
A true sign of respect gained
for you,
In my heart.
It's an inner dialogue
that brings me closer to you.

It's what you do not say
but show it in your actions
that makes me want to trust you
and lead open my guard
bare in front of you.
For I know, you will envelop me
in your care totally
like a warm blanket
does to a person shivering.
It strikes me,
As a realization,
As the melting of my heart,
Which I can now feel so dearly
from within.
I am not sleeping,
I am not dreaming,
I am not in a state of trance,
I am well aware and can feel this clearly.
You here beside me to care,
Why would I fear?
What is there that will cause trouble?
Goosebumps I get from a sheer sense of gladness
which I can now feel so well from within.
Why I didn't realize
that you were there
for me, from the start.
You proved yourself every time,

You taught me the value of
simply being there for someone.
You make me so glad,
I can't help but respect you
for what you made me feel.
You helped me fly.
It wasn't that I wasn't able enough,
but you helped me anyways,
in the ways, my lips can't all tell
but such that
I can definitely feel it
in my heart.
True affections are not forced
but are felt naturally
by the heart.
For its grace
can be felt
by its piousness
that makes it different
than all others.
You don't need to tell me,
I can feel it all the way,
By what you say,
With what intentions,
Which reflects so well
through your actions.
That makes my heart gladdened

to give its token of respect to you,
For you deserve it,
Oh, you so much deserve it.
And now I know
with my mind
without fear
that it is placed in safe hands,
that you have a peep into my heart
and have seen me for real!
Now my heart is lead bare,
For you not afraid to care,
No, I am not sentimental,
I am speaking the truth,
For now,
My heart is speaking,
I am not.
It is giving me this courage from nowhere,
To be with you without any fear,
For you have always made me feel so dear,
Come,
Take my hand,
It's here!

30. GRATITUDE

From the heart of a child in us,

There comes a voice,

So full of life and truth,

The gladness

which one can't hide,

Which shows up

in the sparkle of one's eyes,

and in the smile, that's so natural.

A by-product of a person's care,

A trust that is earned

and a token of respect

that's given back

in return.

In grateful moments

when being treated just right

all negativity disappears

Positivity blossoms.

A vulnerable moment

gratifies the heart,

As the melting snow

it brings an invisible warmth

which one can feel

inside the heart.
Speaking from the heart
A concern showed,
Which we can't pretend.
A moment's care,
An ability to notice the vulnerability,
Not to impress but out of empathy
when we offer,
Melts all doubts,
And on solidifying
creates a bond,
Of trust,
Of being real,
Of an uncompromising respect,
That sprouts out of gratitude
For the other.

.

.

.

.

In the hopes to be able to,
Repay him someday.

31. A PROMISE

Tears welling up in the eyes,
Gladness brimming in the heart,
A promise made while hands in hands,
To stay together, despite all odds
Like no other.

32. A HEARTY TRIBUTE OF GRATITUDE

When truth comes in,
It opens all our eyes,
Transfixes one then and there
To see and behold!
A help offered unsolicited,
It makes eyes shine through tears,
A gush of serene gladness
it runs through one's veins,
Which one can't help
but overflow!
Thus,
Melting down ego,
Cleansing and purifying,
Like a river flowing
from a melting glacier
Leaving behind
coolness and serenity
making the mind calm

a sign of true respect
An emotion so pure,
A mix of sad-glad,
A hearty tribute of gratitude,
Of well-wishing,
For the ones,
Who have earned a place,
Closer to the heart.

33. WAY TOO PURE

Is it true? Or am I blind?
Am I romanticizing the truth?
Or am I being lied to?
Is your beauty true?
Or is it an illusion, a myth?
How can someone be so pure?
Extended sensibilities,
Sensing everything,
Then doing what is right.
Like a lighthouse,
Or a sun shining,
Amidst the black clouds?
Tell, tell me you
O human pure!
How much should I adore?
For thy beauty for me
Is way too pure.
You're an angel
Innocent and pure,
Shows me the path of righteousness,
Guides me through the pitch darkness.
You know me, right?

You have got a great insight,
You help me always like a guide,
How should I thank you?
For your beauty always,
Shines like a diamond, so bright!

34. THE COMMON GROUND

Innocence,
In a world full of wickedness
there you're still
living,
Being yourself.
Here I am
honest,
Living life
carefree,
By staying true
to myself.
On this common ground we both connect,
You naturally being innocent,
And I staying true,
Keeping up
my integrity.
To me it is poetic,
For I can watch and
listen to you
talking, for hours.

For to be able to see
someone being
real and natural both
simultaneously, is rare.
The way I see it,
It inspires me to be
pure and childlike,
Always unaffected
by the surroundings
despite everything.

35. BLESSED

I am indeed much blessed,
Every time I feel I am not being myself
you come to remind me of my true self,
Like a truth that you can
so clearly see from your eyes,
Which makes me want to believe in myself,
Which makes me want to believe in you,
For what you have been towards me
without fail since we have met.
I know I have been stupid
not seeing what has been
in front of me
all along.
But now I have understood
that you are a person genuine,
That you are a person who truly
respect and wish the best for me.
Can't help myself now
but feel your grace,
Which has surfaced
despite the toll of time
like anything.

36. FOR ALL THE TIMES

For all the times you have
respected, believed and listened to what I have said,
For all the times you trusted, were bare and shared,
For all the times you have been
by my side
like an auspicious well-wisher,
For all those times, I promise
I dare, to watch, for you
despite all.
I wonder
for the thing that
made you stay,
For the thing that always
made you believe in me.
You proved yourself
to be the one who deserves
all my heart's affections
that I never showed to you.
Today I am here, standing
with my heart flooding

FOR ALL THE TIMES

with all those affections bare
in front of you.

37. TOGETHERNESS

Togetherness
doesn't require
daily conversations,
But the assurance that
you are there for them
if anytime needed,
Even if you're miles away.
Togetherness
can be felt
just by being
in their company.
No need to speak,
but the assurance that
the other is all ears for you.
When there is a connection,
Their eyes communicate
better than the words.
Listen to all that is being said,
All the while,
Without speaking!

38. CONCERN

Concerns can be felt
In our voice when we talk.
In the matters of the heart
It cannot stay hidden,
It surfaces even by excuse.
We are too shy to tell,
But it doesn't conceal,
What we feel does get communicated.
When affections are real,
They cannot stay hidden for long,
No matter what we speak,
What all the other gets to hear is that -
"I care for you and your well-being".

39. UNCOILING

Build the defences,
Wear the persona,
Be in disguise,
Lie to yourself
and feel safe inside.
But I will come
like the way
a fragrance lingers,
The way a mesh uncoils effortlessly,
When pulled at the right knot.
When someone gets you completely, for you.
Indeed,
There is a way
of communication,
That is more of understanding
and less of speaking,
Which understands,
What we do not speak.
Which prospers,
Faith, comfort and reliability
on the other.
Subtle to feel but has depth,

If only we could understand,
If only we could listen from our heart,
All the ways the other person communicates,
Without actually speaking!
Have you ever felt
The warmth of an understanding pure?
From the moments of extreme passion,
When heart desires are warm,
Feeling together as one,
Hands in hands,
Giving birth to a place
in between us,
That is secure, safe and warm.
A trust is developed,
That has got visions of eternity,
A bond that is felt by us both,
Which gives us some moments of peace,
Despite the outside circumstances,
Irrespective of the talk,
That is being done.
Like as if walking side by side in sync,
Like a music you hear,
Which is so similar to
how you inside feel.
As if uncoiling, unravelling you,
Your heart and your mind,
From the inside.

Making you turn
so light and comfortable
in their presence
as if feathers.
Soothing,
Calming,
Bringing
you
At peace,
From within
Letting you feel
the warmth,
Making you melt
from the inside,
Like an ice cube
placed,
In their palms indeed.
The moments of peace
that you can't forget
how they made you feel
Sprinkling cool droplets of water
over your agitated mind,
Moments when you weren't able to decide
What's wrong and what's right,
Thus, giving you the light,
A calmness serene,
To regain yourself from within!

Like a sunflower facing towards
the direction of the sun,
Gaining its senses lost, now blooming,
Dancing, made beautiful from within.
I owe this inner joy to you,
This way, you connected me with me
A moment of truth,
Of understanding can shed,
All the clouds of doubt that gather over,
Your mind and soul.
Making you believe in the thing
which can't be seen by your eyes,
But it can only be felt
By your heart within!
So silently I pray,
Wherever you are just listen bae,
The songs of innocence are what am I singing,
To cherish the present moments of bliss.
For I don't know, neither do I wish to know
what the future will unfold,
See I am kind first, then bold,
Found you once on that blissful day,
And now every day,
In front of the almighty above,
For your well-being, here do I pray.

40. ONE

Warmth brimming,
Affection
empathy
compassion
kindness,
All coming out
from one's heart gladness,
A sense of serene sadness
that will provoke one to tears,
Melting of our heart we will see,
Tears coming out of an extreme glee,
Beyond hold,
A total surrender,
Unifying,
The two
Into ONE.

41. AFFECTIONS

Like a flower that we touch
and caress gently,
My affections for you come
in the similar way,
To cup your face
in between the palms of my hands,
Or being concerned,
Listening to you
unfolding yourself
in front of me
slowly and gradually
Like a piece of art!

42. TRUE CONCERN

Do you notice?
How I adore you,
By just listening,
Like a calmness serene,
That tells you without me speaking
"Don't worry; everything will be fine!"
For I have seen beauty in this world,
For I know the meaning of a kind gesture,
For you know what it takes to offer,
For you know how noble it is,
"A single act of love"
Of compassion,
Of doing nothing,
Yet everything that one needs,
To make his heart lightened.
A moment of peace
To be!
Like the first ray of the sun,
Filling you with the warmth,
Turning your sad face into glee,
And thus, in those moments
All the miseries flee!

All the miseries flee!
The fact that one cares
and the other person matters
doesn't require communication skills
or big speeches/letters for its proof.
It can be felt in one's eyes,
In one's true concern.
Which can be felt in the heart
by the other.
For its purity transcends
the need for words...

43. AN UNDERSTANDING

I see the pain fading,
I see the air flowing,
I see you as you become
as calm as a sea!
I see the wind flowing,
Asking us to flow,
To never hold on,
To never stop rather keep flowing.
I see you, as you speak softly into my ears,
I see you, as you want to embrace the silence
which now feels comforting.
I see as we melt again,
I see as we become humane
from a person insane
without a stain,
Pure,
At peace,
Inside our minds.
Leave the train of thought
and rest in my arms

for a while,
And maybe
<u>Smile.</u>
For understanding warrants
a natural therapeutic response
in silence that comprehends
the feelings
that only you and I appreciate,
If either must explain
or articulate in a situation
like this,
It surely leaves a sour taste,
For the sensitivity is lost.

44. SILENT LOVE

Love unravelled,
You to me,
And from me to you,
It travelled.
Melting my heart
your silent gestures
you see,
Tone of my voice
putting you at an ease
I see,
Here now all troubles
seems to flee,
And opening a door
to enter in between us,
glee.
Happiness is finding someone
out from the crowd with whom
you could be just you!
I don't need to speak,
Look into my eyes
and tell me aren't they saying
all I ever want to say to you?

Feel me now,
For I feel you,
Let me be me,
I let you be you.
Have you ever wanted to talk a lot
but without speaking a single word?
To speak in feelings
as they come
Talking, as if thinking out loud
No filter,
No fear,
An understanding,
A silence,
Which speaks volumes,
If only one cares enough
to listen,
To see the unseen.
A sacred connection
which sprouts faith
for the other,
To be there
carrying
in silence
the warmth,
Only
for us
to feel

from
within.
Silence is beautiful, very beautiful
if we could just look into each other's eyes
and read all we ever want to say.
What I say doesn't matter,
but how I say it, is hypnotising indeed.
Can one sit silently in someone's company
and never feel bored?
Gladness is a silent gesture of a melting heart,
Melting all other pains together as well
making one feel good.
Like the effervescence of
or a sip from the green tea,
Which improves our mood
and gives us peace.

45. A STILLNESS

Sipping coffee from the corner of my cup
as I see
a stillness comes into me.
At first
you seem to be at an unease
but all of a sudden
you too begin to feel
the same stillness as me.
I keep looking over you as I was,
To finally see my careful calm stillness
To break the glass
To leap into you
who I was,
And so, you too begin
to lock your eyes with me,
Can't express what a connection it felt
when you did so in between,
Felt as if the whole world
has stopped for a while,
Just to watch our conversational style,
Me and you and no one else to bother,
We two seem connected

while the whole world
seems to be lost rather,
That's the true connection
for which I always long,
I talk to a few but when I do
I get completely involved,
Being lost in the convo
feels so amazing,
I bet this connection can't be felt
in a group or in any other facing,
Can't compare this connection with any other,
It feels as if we two have become one together.
Don't know how
but indeed, I have
an innate ability of this,
To hold such deep, meaningful conversations
for hours and hours without a release,
Without even having a slightest bit of unease,
Rather this sort of convo brings
the other person at ease,
Out of nowhere they feel inclined,
As if slowly and gradually
they are losing their head
and becoming blind,
Their whole attention
seems to converge into me,
Whatever they offer

I absorb it completely,
By offerings I mean to say
whatever they felt like sharing
keeping their fears at the bay,
At that moment
they feel as if I am
the safest reservoir available
with whom they can get
their deepest secrets laid.
Wish you too someday
may get to feel
the same connection as I feel,
With whosoever that you may stay,
Who at first seems to be at a bay
but soon starts to unfold
his/her life to you
as the connection in between you two
<u>Starts to build up anyway.</u>

46. A DEEPER CONNECTION

If I am blessed with
an ability to express
I would let you know
somewhat I couldn't explain as such
but what I can't help but behold
in the moment.
Feelings,
Sentiments,
Vibes,
Connect me to you.
Weather,
Nature,
Speaks,
Its silent verses,
All the time to us.
Talk with me,
In the similar way.
Let's connect,
On a level deeper.
Somewhat that

is sanctioned
by a trust gained
and a gratitude felt
in the heart of us both,
Which clears all our doubts
and lets moments of
peace and gladness
to seep in us
when we are together.
The moments
when one is drawn in,
A warmth is felt,
when spoken in words
soft as whispers,
To melt away,
To feel together,
Beating as one.
Same
In sync,
As if getting inside
each other skins,
Feeling as one.
Like a puzzle
whose pathway
now only we can see
so clearly.
As if the truth

Now lead bare,
Only for us
To behold,
To be,
In the moment.

47. TRUE CONNECTIONS

Freedom,
A sense of belonging
and openness that one feels
which reflects,
How dear they are to you.
An understanding offered
unasked,
And a trust that leaves one bare
just the way one is,
With fear replaced by faith,
And no duality in the mind
for the other.
Connections which are true and pure
can be felt in the heart.
Makes one feel loved and solved.
A reliability which knows no bounds,
And makes one feel connected
despite everything.
Indeed, a sense of belonging
is all that we need,

*To sail through everything
that life throws at us.*

48. SHARED LIFE

Life becomes easier,
When we feel
that we belong.
A safe place to lean on to,
Which gives us peace and confidence
amidst the chaos.
To go straight into
the storms of life
without fear.
Or to nurture other life,
To live for another soul,
To share our journey with,
To feel that we belong,
And are not,
All alone.
Life when shared
gives itself meaning.
Shared life is indeed
the grease of life.

49. TO CALL SOMEONE YOURS

Someone,
Whom we don't think twice before
holding their hands and calling them ours.
Someone,
Who gives us the feelings of permanence
despite the reality of our mortal and unpredictable lives.
Someone,
With whom we can give a rest to our running.
Someone,
Who becomes the treasure of life itself.
To live and cherish along.
Togetherness brings warmth and intimacy.
A sort of feeling that sweeps away,
All sorts of anxieties, fears and doubts of our mind.
The flower of love blossoms
To envelope us whole.
United, this unity brings
peace to our heart and mind
and makes our life simply,
A treasure worth sharing with someone.

With equivalence and transparency,
This shared life,
Makes one feel grateful to simply be,
It makes one feel that
despite everything
that life throws at us,
As long as
we have got each other's back,
This life, Ah! It remains beautiful.

50. GLIMMER

Maybe simple was enough,
Maybe it is all we seek
at the day's end,
When eyes don't glare,
Desiring intimacy to share.
Now when I look back,
They all seem so precious,
Glimmer, dazzling eyes
Social media took all away,
The beauty, the gladness,
Of small joys forever.

51. HUMAN TOUCH

I know the unspoken
yet so sound ways
in which warmth of affection and
a sense of belonging is felt.
It melts the ice between the two,
Making them feel safe and trusted
by each other.
An unspoken but unmistakable indication
that one enjoys the other's company.
When pure,
are meant to be shown and felt
and never repressed,
Due to any uncertain,
unethical fear or embarrassment
of crossing the line.
For the simple warmth of a human touch,
Can speak volumes of what
one couldn't explain
in just words.

52. WARMTH

When hearts are together
words become irrelevant,
The two experience
a feeling of composure
in the language of silence
Otherwise,
Even an embrace feels
A loathsome aversion,
Akin to invading a foreign land,
Obnoxiously.
If my intentions have been true,
If my concerns have been pure,
And if you feel that
you have known me enough to
know that I am a person
that can be trusted,
Hereby I offer my touch.
A touch to touch you,
To show that I care,
To melt and unite together,
In that shared warmth and intimacy
As One.

53. SO CLOSE TO ME

Feather running along my temples,
Making me tickle
as if teasing me,
I lower down my eyes
with a smile at my face
and find myself in goosebumps.
Is this an essence of your touch?
or is this just your presence?
That's making me blush!
I have an adrenaline rushing
through my veins,
Cold fingers,
Heavy breathing,
My eyes linger
through my hood,
Looking at you,
<u>So close to me!</u>

54. INNOCENCE LOST

It's slightly mature how
innocence gets lost.
Slowly and gradually
like an onion being peeled,
Layer by layer
Or as if,
Your clothes are being removed,
One by one.
A vision,
A desire,
To taste it,
The hidden bliss.
Let the desires take flight
not in the wings of imagination anymore,
But for real.
When Rumi said -
"When you remove all sense of self
the bonds of a thousand chains will vanish"
I never thought of it this way as well.
But now,

You find yourself free
as you look into
the other person's eyes
without any hint of
sense of shame or hesitation,
But when together as you bake
the inner desires true.
Innocence lost,
In a slightly mature way.
The chain unlocked,
Now you find yourself in touch,
By touching the other,
All that you want to!

55. COME TO ME

So softly I say
just listen bae,
Here I lay,
Pull the curtains,
And in the darkness
we would
set our souls
On fire
with heart's desires,
Pure and honest ones,
You feel me
I feel you,
You love me
like the way you do,
Me here
completely bare,
It melts my tensions
your loving embrace,
Love me,
Come to me babe.

56. DESIRES INFLAMES

Desire inflames
I can see my muse
in front of me
mesmerizing
guiding me
to the bliss
to taste it,
Bewitched I am
following your directions.
You're like a nerve stretched
inside my heart,
It vibrates my insides
like as if guitar strings.
Place your head in my chest
and listen to my heartbeats as they raise,
Feel the pulse, the throbbing of my veins,
Feel the heat, here tonight when we two meet,
In the dim lights, under the bed sheets,
Guide me show me the ways,
As my vision is now in haze,

And here I find myself gazing at your face,
Telling me to be more,
Let's find out what's there in store,
The time to melt our pains,
The time for you to trust my ways,
For I am here for you babe,
Look into my eyes and see,
*In your arms…**Here I am laid!***

57. IN THE OVEN OF TONIGHT FIRES

Feel my comfort
Soft as whispers,
Turning mind melodious,
Eyes flirtatious,
Tonight, be jovial gracious,
In the bedsheets of silk we lay,
Drink from my cup I say,
In the darkness of night
we ignite in between us the light
keeping troubles at a bay,
Feel me as I can feel you,
Let's put together and bake our desires
in the oven of tonight fires,
Feel the heat when together here we two meet,
Our heart drum beats rhythmically
Soaring high moods, we can't cheat.
Look me in the eye and see,
Tonight, I ain't shy,
Who, where, when and why today,
All questions are going to die.

Nobody can put off tonight this heat,
When with brimming passion here we two meet.
Set the rhythm, set the pace,
Take the helm in your hands
of our ship moving forward
on our body seas,
Guide me, be without any fear
For I am here
in front of you,
To take care,
To be bare,
To unite,
To be,
As One,
My dear.

58. A TEST

Being terrified of the thought,
The girl asked to the boy :
"If I ever lose my beauty,
Would you still cherish me the way you did?
Filled with wonder, with my natural gift.
Will you come close, make love to me and still admire?
Or would you simply neglect me and retire?"
A question that questions your nature true,
Are you really a person kind?
Or just another selfish dude.
I have been the brightest,
And I have been the faintest,
If you can stick with me during both,
If you can call me "mine" when the world declines,
If you can lift me up when the rainy days comes,
If you could prove to me that you really care,
Then my lover, with you, my beauty
I will always share.

59. PICTURE PERFECT

Picture perfect beauty
Are we looking through it?
To hear the unspoken,
To see the unseen,
To know the unknown,
Hidden yet is visible,
If only we can look past through,
The transient beauty
and speak to her
to reach to her soul,
To know her for real.
To embrace the true beauty
that shines through,
Like Sunbeams,
Unfettered!

60. THE ETERNAL BEAUTY

Bells chiming,
Ice cool winter weathers here,
Sound of horses trotting by
While pulling horse carts there,
Dark mesmerizing
Chocolaty aroma all around,
It seems as if I've managed
to go back to Old England! for sure.
The beauty of this place is alluring,
Then, all of a sudden
I notice,
My eyes stuck on a girl,
Who is passing by there.
As silent as a lake is her face.
Like the first ray of sun
Is the shine in her eyes.
Earrings of hers chime
As if they are bells in shrines.
The way sunlight shimmers there
Through the curtain of oak trees

Her dress shines in the same way.
Her scent resembles
With the chocolaty aroma.
It feels as if
She does belong to that place no?
Her footsteps make sounds
Like that of a horse, trotting by.
Complexion of hers
Is like moonlight.
Her red fingernails
are like thorns of a rose
which seem to warn those
who wishes to harm the beauty of hers.
Like a blanket are, her hair,
I wish to go and talk
let her know of all the beauty
which she possesses.
But then, all of a sudden, I realise
All that glitters, is not gold
One day, as she is human
She too will get old!
All those Oak trees
will too face the autumn.
All that shimmering sunlight of winters
will too turn to scorching heat of summers.
The Red fingernails of hers
will too one day fell off

just like rose petals.
Those shiny eyes, will too one day
lose proper sight.
That white skin, will too one day
become pale and dull.
The silence at her face
will too may bear hues and cries.
Those Flowing hair of hers
Which seemed, like a blanket
Will too one day, litter around
As if they're torn pages.
That mesmerizing smell of hers
Will too one day start stinking
Like that of mud!
Here I am, waiting,
For that very day,
When all those glitters
that successfully misguided many
will reveal their bitter truth to everyone.
On this day I will embrace
The Real Beauty of hers,
Which will never fade,
Even by a slightest bit, ever.
Rather, it will stay with her
All along from cradle, to grave.
Beauty of her heart,
Beauty of her soul,

Which forever remains
young and warm,
Even at the time,
When her outer beauty,
Seems to start melting,
With wrinkles!

Previews

AN AFFECTIONATE READ

At first, I couldn't believe that a boy in this era of hook-up culture was thinking and feeling so deeply for someone. It was not easy to digest, but when we read, we imagine our own lover saying the words for us. It seemed as if my ex was the one writing for me. He is showering love on me. Which does not exist in reality but through these pages. We always used to say we and us while we were together, and I could feel that togetherness while reading these poems.

The tone of the poems was very soft and humble. It was very clear, crisp, and soulful to read. I felt more of an authentic writer vibe from the poems. It was something I didn't expect but was actually written out. Just like it is in qawwalis, where there is deep meaning but zero rhyming.

In simple words, it is a mix of emotions, the ability to isolate while feeling the same emotion without expecting anything in return, selflessness, and peace.

True humanity could be sensed the entire time I read each poem.

To learn about love and let go at the same time will never be easy, but it will always be easy to pour out in the form of poetry, and I think that is what the beauty of this book is. So pious to get rid of.

Some of my favourite poems in the book were :

To call someone yours : This was my personal favourite.

In the oven of tonight's fires : This gave me the essence of warmth.

True companionship : This one had peace from both sides.

- Neha Singhal, Research Scholar, Writer, Educator, New Delhi

A LOVE LETTER TO LIFE

Neeraj Kumar's anthology, "For All The Times," is a poetic masterpiece that captures the essence of life's blissful moments. The compilation of poems is an intricate tapestry of reflections that inspire deep contemplation and soulful reflection. With a rare gift of language, Neeraj crafts poems that resonate with themes of love, companionship, memories, gratitude, and serenity.

Each verse in this collection is a love letter to life, and the imagery used is so vivid that it transports the reader to a realm of pure joy. Neeraj's love for nature shines through his words. With each poem, he invites the reader to revel in the beauty of the world and share in his profound appreciation for life's gifts.

In "For All The Times," Neeraj explores the different facets of human connection, emphasizing the importance of cherishing every moment spent with loved ones. He captures the essence of true companionship that make every connection special. Through his words, he reminds us of the power of human connection and the joy that comes from nurturing relationships.

Overall, "For All The Times" is an awe-inspiring collection of poems that uplifts the spirit and nourishes the soul. With a masterful use of language, Neeraj has created an anthology that inspires gratitude, joy, and appreciation for life's blessings. This collection is a must-read for anyone seeking to discover the beauty and wonder of the world around them.

- Tijan Sanutee Kabbah Jr., A Student Leader, Writer, and Generational Thinker, Monrovia-Liberia, West Africa

FOR ROMANTICS OF ALL AGES

"For All The Times" by Neeraj Kumar is an outstanding poetry collection of love poems. Neeraj writes with clear emotional depth and with the ability to capture beautiful verses expressing love in all its wonderful forms, making this book relatable to whoever is reading.

All the poems touch the heart in one way or another, love is a universal language and Neeraj speaks it beautifully for we've all felt that incredible rush of new love or experienced an amazing crush of attraction, or succumbed to deep emotional commitment.

Finally, "For All The Times' is a poetry collection you will be happy to place on your night to revisit many times over. A must-read for romantics of all ages!

- TM DiSarro, Port Charlotte, Florida USA, Author of two books. Poet predominantly

SECULAR PSALMS

I have no words... actually, I do have two:

Secular Psalms!

1) Secular because they revered humans (not negatively).

Neeraj Kumar's words are not "fantasy," but realistic, bare, and so open; they're attractive to you, not for their perfection, but for their being themselves, unique, and generally attractive. The voice is so appealing, informing them of how they make you feel—not sensual but whole.

2) Psalms (poems of similar nature) because the flow is more like a verse continuation than different headings.

Tone is like "ancient love," referencing things that matter like their grace, company, innocence, nobility, respectful nature, honesty, etc.

The language is simple, clear, and respectful.

- Faith Luke, Young Poetess, Kenya

A FASCINATING READ

Firstly, I really liked the title and about the book page, which gave me an idea of what to expect (well, practically, a good reader should not make presumptions, but I guess I was looking forward to a person's diary of poems throughout his relationship.)

There were a collection of long and short poems with along with free verse. I was fascinated as to how a lot of them had questions in them and how each of it was a unique story in its own.

I don't know why I distinguishably remember the poem "TEST"... maybe because having reading just one person's perceptive, it suddenly felt fresh and relatable when poem started with a question by her. Well, all poems are very realistic in this book. It was a pleasure reading your poems.

- Ekta Agrawal, Avid reader, Student from Delhi

Thank You Note

Thanks for taking time to read my words.

If my words have rung true to you in any way, if my poems somehow brought a smile to your face and helped you recall the blissful moments spent with the significant other of your life, I would be grateful if you spared a minute to put a review on the Amazon website.

You're All Amazing,

Your Well Wisher,

Neeraj Kumar

About The Poet

<u>Neeraj Kumar (aka penmatician)</u> is a young literature enthusiast, an avid reader, a poet, and a writer from New Delhi, India. He has a keen interest in spiritual and philosophical books; as they simply broaden the perspective of his life. The majority of his writings are life-affirming. They mostly revolve around compassion, humanity, love, and the warmth of human relationships.

He has also co-authored a Self-Help book titled **"Conquer Yourself"** with Shyam Kumar. It is available on Amazon in paperback and Kindle format. He has also been able to go international with his anthology with STRIDA (Nigeria), with the title "Kiss at Last: To the Tired Flames."

Apart from literature, he likes to spend quality time with his close friends. He is also very fond of music, movies and food blogging in his free time.

You can follow him on Instagram on : -

1) **penmatician** - His writing page and also his pen name.

2) **foodieneeraj** - His food and travel blogging page on Instagram.